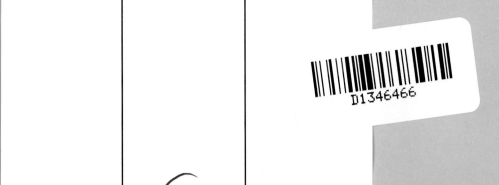

C

HT

Please renew or return items by the date
shown on your receipt

www.hertfordshire.gov.uk/libraries

Renewals and enquiries: 0300 123 4049

Textphone for hearing or 0300 123 4041
speech impaired users:

L32 11.16

Hertfordshire

Chineasy®
FOR CHILDREN

by SHAOLAN 曉嵐
with illustrations by NOMA BAR

Thames & Hudson

hello

Chineasy is the fun and easy way to learn how to read Chinese with pictures. I developed Chineasy because I wanted to teach my children one of the most complicated languages in the world! This effective system helps children to lay the foundation to reach basic Chinese literacy quickly.

Chinese doesn't have an a-z of letters that make up words, like the English language. The Chinese language has symbols called characters – thousands of them. It can be tough remembering them all. Most of the characters in this book are called simplified characters. To find out more about the origins of traditional and simplified characters, go to page 78.

This book shows children how to remember even tricky characters by imagining them as pictures. 100 of the basic and useful characters are grouped into favourite themes, including the body, animals, and nature. The more characters children learn, the more characters they can make. And that's what makes Chineasy so very easy.

ShaoLan 曉嵐

what's inside?

reading pictures

This book is full of pictures called characters. The Chinese language is made up of thousands of characters. It doesn't use letters to make words like the English language.

Every time you see a picture in this book, look at the shape of the black lines. This shape is the Chinese character.

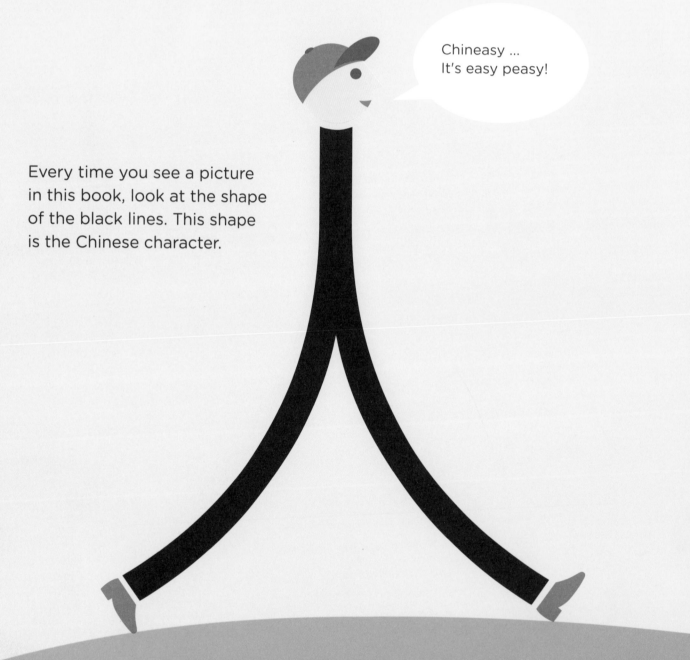

Chineasy ...
It's easy peasy!

Can you guess from the picture what this Chinese character means? It looks like two long legs. This is the character for **person**.

1

2

Trace your finger over the black lines.
First trace downwards from number 1,
then downwards from number 2.

Look at the black lines of the character for **tree**. They look like a trunk and thick branches.

This is the character for **tree** without the picture.

tree
mù

This shows how to pronounce the word in Chinese. Go to page 75 to find out how to make the different sounds.

writing Chinese

In China, children practise drawing characters neatly inside boxes, again and again. For each character, the lines, called strokes, are drawn in a particular order and direction. In this box, the numbers show the order to write the strokes for **tree**.

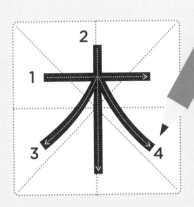

The character for **woods** is two trees.

The character for **forest** is three trees.

woods
lín

forest
sēn

common characters

The Chinese characters for these really useful words have been used since ancient times.

follow the clues ...

Look at each picture and guess what the character means. Follow the clues to help. Then pair up each picture with its matching character at the bottom of the page.

'I've got a trunk and branches.'

'I can walk and talk.'

Stand outside and look up!

Drip! Drip!

water
shuǐ

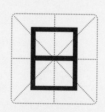

sun
rì

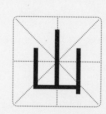

mountain
shān

moon
yuè

'My flames dance upwards.'

Climb to the top. Phew!

'I shine through a window at night.'

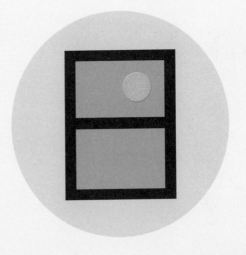

'I shine through a window in the daytime.'

sky
tiān

tree
mù

person
rén

fire
huǒ

go to **page 80** for answers

building words

There are three types of Chineasy characters. They are called a building block character, a compound character and a phrase.

building block character

The character for **person** is a building block character. It helps to make many new characters. How will you remember this character? Does it look like a **person** walking to you?

compound character

The compound character for **big** is based on the building block character for **person**. It looks like a person with their arms stretched out wide.

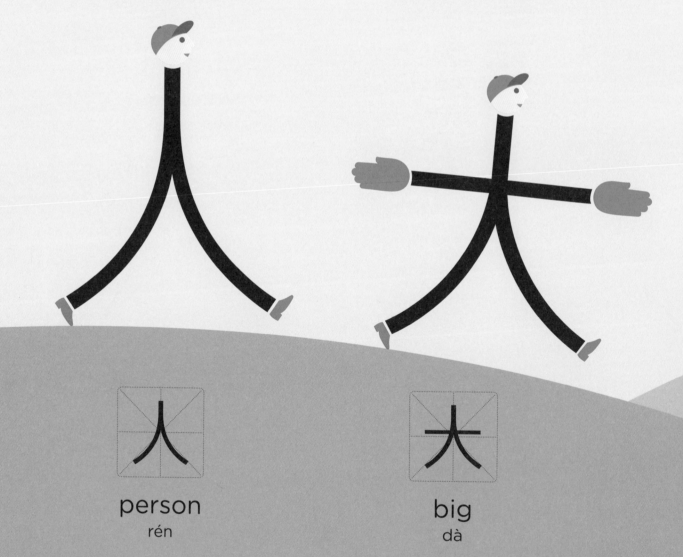

person
rén

big
dà

One box shows it is either a building block character or a compound character.

phrase

When you put the characters for **big** and **person** side by side, they connect to make the character for **adult**. When connecting characters sit next to each other, they make a phrase.

This says **adult.**

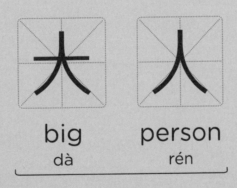

big
dà

person
rén

adult
dà rén

Two boxes shows it is a phrase.

building new characters

Once you're familiar with a few building block characters, you will start to recognise their shapes in compound characters. Play spot the difference between the two.

compound characters

A building block character can turn into a compound character.

Take the building block character for **person**, add wide shoulders and long arms to make the compound character **man.**

person
rén

man
fū

Spot the difference between the building block character **sun** and the compound character **sunrise**. For **sunrise** imagine a window ledge and the **sun** rising.

man and **sunrise** are compound characters. Each sits in one box.

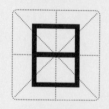

sun
rì

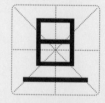

sunrise
dàn

phrases

When connecting characters sit next to each other, they make a new word, called a phrase.

人 + 魚 = 人魚
mermaid
rén yú

人
person
rén

魚
fish
yú

火 + 山 = 火山
volcano
huǒ shān

火
fire
huǒ

山
mountain
shān

mermaid and **volcano** are phrases. A phrase sits in two or more boxes.

What do you think this Chinese proverb means?

A happy heart has a cheerful face.

Proverbs are wise sayings about how to live a good life. The meaning of a proverb is not always clear and it takes careful thought to find the answer.

my world

body

top to toe

Answer these clues by matching up the Chinese characters with the pictures.

'I kick a football with my ....'

'I lick an ice-cream with my ...'

'I hold a pencil in my ...'

Make up more clues and play this game with a friend.

go to **page 80** for answers

足
foot
zú

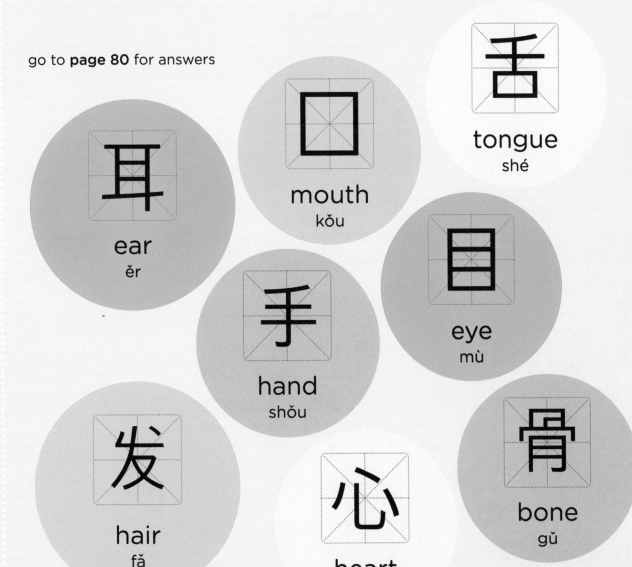

舌
tongue
shé

口
mouth
kǒu

耳
ear
ěr

目
eye
mù

手
hand
shǒu

发
hair
fǎ

心
heart
xīn

骨
bone
gǔ

family

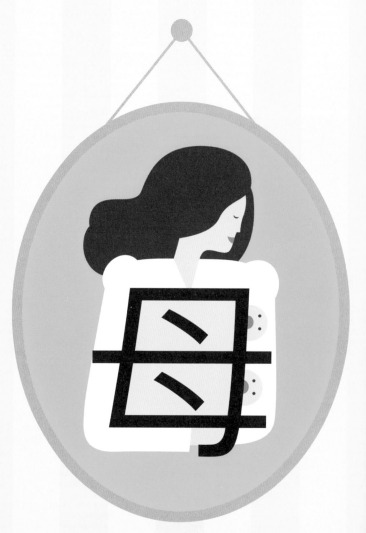

father
fù

mother
mǔ

子

son
zǐ

女

**daughter
or woman**
nǚ

chop chop

Find the shape of two axes crossed
together in the Chinese character
for **father**. This character comes
from long ago, when it was common
for a man to chop wood with an
axe to make a fire for his family.

king and queen

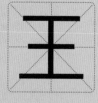

king
wáng

take a bow

In ancient times, an emperor ruled China. When you met this all-powerful ruler, you had to bow and touch your forehead right to the floor as a sign of respect.

后

queen
hòu

people

ghost
guǐ

clown
chǒu

witch
wū

soldier
shì

balloon spotting

Answer these questions by pointing to the Chinese character on the balloons.

'I wear a hat and I'm spooky. Which colour balloon am I?'

'I'm the only one without a hat. I'm also spooky. Which colour balloon am I?'

go to **page 80** for answers

opposites

big
dà

small
xiǎo

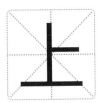

up
shàng

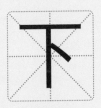

who's where?

The lifts are going up and down. Is the Chinese character for **big** in the **up** or **down** lift?

go to **page 80** for the answer

down
xià

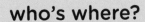

counting to ten

六
six
liù

七
seven
qī

八
eight
bā

一
one
yī

二
two
èr

三
three
sān

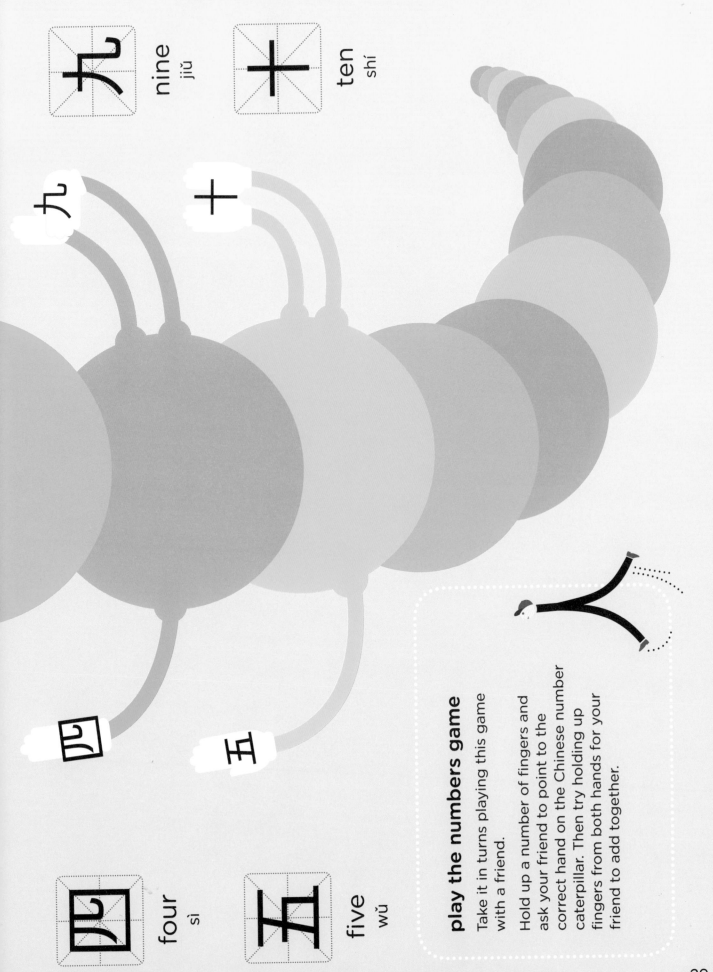

九 nine
jiǔ

十 ten
shí

四 four
sì

五 five
wǔ

play the numbers game

Take it in turns playing this game with a friend.

Hold up a number of fingers and ask your friend to point to the correct hand on the Chinese number caterpillar. Then try holding up fingers from both hands for your friend to add together.

What do you think this Chinese proverb means?

A greedy person is like a snake who wants to swallow an elephant.

animals

象

on the farm

clip clop

Find the shape of four legs and a swishing tail in the Chinese character for **horse**.

牛
cow
niú

兔
rabbit
tù

32

馬
horse
mǎ

鸡
chicken
jī

豬

羊
sheep
yáng

豬
pig
zhū

33

pets

貓

cat

māo

狗

狗

dog

gǒu

lucky animals

Since ancient times, Chinese people have linked luck and happiness to certain animals. A dog is thought to be friendly and loyal.

go to **page 58** to find out about animals in the **Chinese zodiac**

pond life

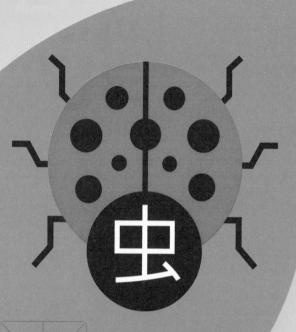

鳥

鳥

bird
niǎo

虫

bug
chóng

蛙

蛙

frog
wā

duck

yā

turtle

guī

guess who?

Answer these questions by pointing to the Chinese characters in the picture.

'I make my home inside a hard brown shell with a pattern on top. What am I?'

'We are the same kind of animal. We both have feathers. What are we?'

go to **page 80** for answers

fish

yú

in the wild

熊
bear
xióng

蛇

蛇
snake
shé

watch out!

Imagine the **snake** hissing and flicking its tongue in and out. What story will you make up to remember the shape of the Chinese character for **deer** or another animal in the picture?

虎 虎
tiger
hǔ

人

38

鹿

鹿
deer
lù

象

猴
monkey
hóu

猴

象
elephant
xiàng

What do you think this Chinese proverb means?

When you walk on snow, you can't hide your footprints.

nature

nature walk

soil
tǔ

deeply rooted

Imagine the Chinese character for **soil** as a little seedling with its roots in the soil and its stalk poking up above the ground.

羽

feather
yǔ

貝

shell
bèi

草
grass
cǎo

山
mountain
shān

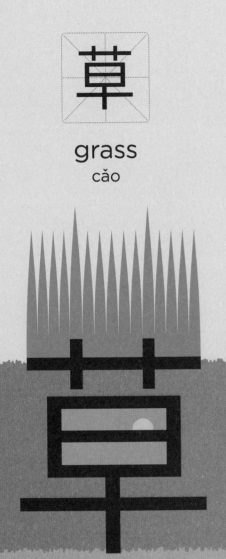

石

石
stone
shí

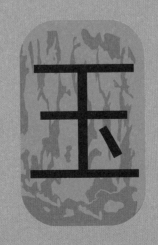
玉
jade
yù

weather

cloud
yún

snow
xuě

feathery snow

The ancient Chinese thought snow looked like feathers falling from the sky. Today, when there are big snowflakes, people say, 'It's snowing like goose feathers'.

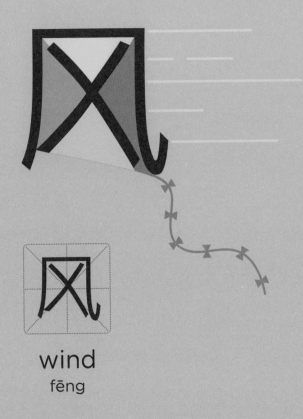

风

wind

fēng

雨

rain

yǔ

鴨

sun and moon

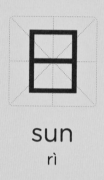

sun
rì

sunrise
dàn

月
moon
yuè

夕
sunset
xī

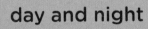

day and night
Imagine the Chinese character
for **sun** as a big glass window.
What story will you make up
to remember the character for
moon?

the planets

planets and stars

The ancient Chinese believed the five elements, or forces, of gold, wood, water, fire and soil ruled everything, including the planets.

The names of the planets seen from Earth are all made in the same way from two characters. Look at how Jupiter's name is made. The first character is **wood**, which also means **tree**. The second character is **star**.

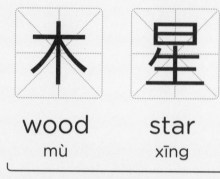

木
wood
mù

星
star
xīng

Jupiter
mù xīng

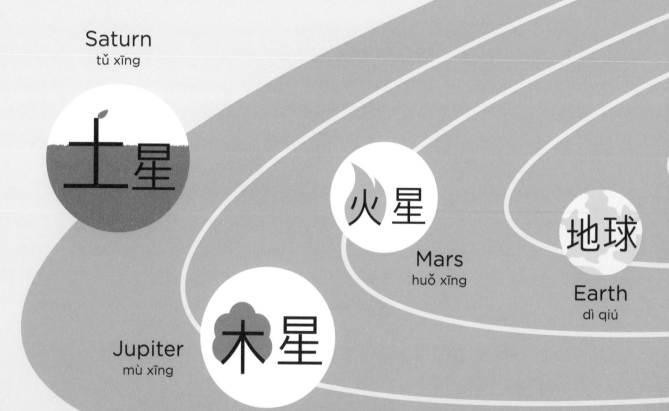

Saturn
tǔ xīng

土星

Mars
huǒ xīng

火星

Earth
dì qiú

地球

Jupiter
mù xīng

木星

star spotting

Look at the planets in the picture.
Match up each planet with its name below.

fire star   **water star**   **wood star**

soil star   **gold star**

go to **page 80** for answers

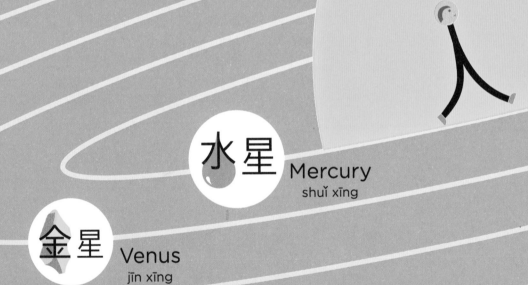

水星 Mercury
shuǐ xīng

金星 Venus
jīn xīng

What do you think this Chinese proverb means?

A long journey always starts with a first step.

let's go
to China

China

Over 1 billion people live in China – more than in any country in the world. There are towering cities, small villages, green forests and snowy mountains.

let's explore

Match up each Chinese character in this box with a picture on the map.

capital
jīng

river
chuān

forest
sēn

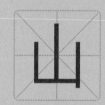

mountain
shān

sea
hǎi

boat
zhōu

Mount Everest is the highest **mountain** in the world. It's 8,848 m high.

go to **page 80** for answers

Beijing is the **capital** of China.

The longest **river** in China is the Yangtze River. It's 6,300 km long.

Shanghai

Yangtze River

noodle bar

米
rice
mǐ

面
noodle
miàn

茶
tea
chá

肉

meat

ròu

birthday slurp

In China, it's a tradition that a birthday boy or girl eats really long noodles, and then makes a big slurping sound! People think long noodles are lucky and a sign of a long and happy life ahead.

Imagine your favourite noodle dish sitting on top of the Chinese character for **noodle**.

瓜

melon

guā

果

fruit

guǒ

dragon boat festival

let's race

Every year in China a festival is held at the seaside with boats decorated to look like fierce dragons. Teams of sailors from local villages race the boats across the water.

舟

龙

人

鳥

車

貝

貝

postcard match-up

Match each of these Chinese characters to a picture in the festival.

boat
zhōu

dragon
lóng

car
chē

sea
hǎi

bird
niǎo

shell
bèi

go to **page 80** for answers

zodiac animals

magic in the sky

The Chinese zodiac is an imaginary strip of sky high above our heads. Many people believe the zodiac has magical powers.

Here's a story about how it all began.

Long before clocks measured time, an emperor ruled that the calendar would be organised around twelve animals. But which animal would come first? The emperor held a race across the river to decide.

Cat and Rat were best friends. They weren't good at swimming so asked Cow to take them across the river. Cow was kind and agreed.

On race morning, Rat deliberately didn't wake up his best friend Cat. So Cow and Rat set off by themselves ...

豬
豬
pig
zhū

狗
狗
dog
gǒu

鸡
鸡
chicken
jī

猴
猴
monkey
hóu

羊
sheep
yáng

羊

馬
horse
mǎ

馬

貓

... Just as Cow was about to reach the other side of the river, Rat quickly jumped off Cow's back and landed on the river bank, then dashed over the finishing line. Rat won the race!

The order of the zodiac was decided and Cat wasn't included. Cat was very cross and fought with Rat from then on.

Each year is named after one of the twelve zodiac animals. Many Chinese people believe that the year you are born helps to shape your luck and happiness.

鼠
rat
shǔ

牛
cow
niú

虎
tiger
hǔ

兔
rabbit
tù

龙
dragon
lóng

蛇
snake
shé

Chinese New Year

Let's celebrate

At Chinese New Year, families celebrate with delicious feasts. Everyone likes to dress up in new clothes and wear gold jewellery. In the streets, there are paper-dragon parades and fireworks.

party match-up

Match up each New Year picture on the opposite page with a Chinese character on this page.

go to **page 80** for answers

子

金

果

米

肉

魚

母

龙

父

女

What do you think this Chinese proverb means?

The road to a friend's house is never long.

picture dictionary

characters

Here are all the Chinese characters from this book. Which ones do you remember?

body

耳
ear
ěr

目
eye
mù

发
hair
fǎ

口
mouth
kǒu

舌
tongue
shé

手
hand
shǒu

足
foot
zú

心
heart
xīn

骨
bone
gǔ

people

人
person
rén

夫
man
fū

母
mother
mǔ

父
father
fù

子
son
zǐ

女
daughter or woman
nǚ

go to **page 80** for the answer

I spy with my little eye ...
... a Chinese character on these pages that looks like a big person with outstretched arms walking. Can you guess the answer?

food

王
king
wáng

后
queen
hòu

茶
tea
chá

米
rice
mǐ

丑
clown
chǒu

鬼
ghost
guǐ

面
noodle
miàn

肉
meat
ròu

巫
witch
wū

士
soldier
shì

果
fruit
guǒ

瓜
melon
guā

characters

animals

牛

cow
niú

兔

rabbit
tù

鸡

chicken
jī

馬

horse
mǎ

羊

sheep
yáng

豬

pig
zhū

貓

cat
māo

狗

dog
gǒu

虫

bug
chóng

鳥

bird
niǎo

蛙

frog
wā

鴨

duck
yā

go to **page 80** for the answer

I spy with my little eye ...
... GRRR!, an animal with a huge roar. The Chinese character also has marks like long sharp teeth. Can you guess the answer?

龜

turtle
guī

魚

fish
yú

Your turn

Take it in turns to play I Spy with a friend. First choose an animal character. Don't tell your friend which one you've chosen. What clues will you give? When you friend guesses right, it's his or her turn.

蛇

snake
shé

熊

bear
xióng

虎

tiger
hǔ

鹿

deer
lù

猴

monkey
hóu

象

elephant
xiàng

鼠

rat
shǔ

龙

dragon
lóng

characters

nature

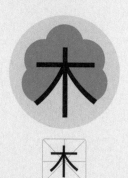

木
tree
mù

林
woods
lín

森
forest
sēn

火
fire
huǒ

山
mountain
shān

水
water
shuǐ

月
moon
yuè

日
sun
rì

旦
sunrise
dàn

夕
sunset
xī

海
sea
hǎi

天
sky
tiān

go to **page 80** for the answer

人

I spy with my little eye ...
... a Chinese character
on these pages that looks
like dancing flames.
Can you guess the answer?

貝
shell
bèi

土
soil
tǔ

羽
feather
yǔ

草
grass
cǎo

石
stone
shí

玉
jade
yù

云
cloud
yún

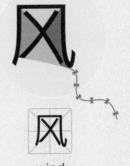
风
wind
fēng

雨
rain
yǔ

雪
snow
xuě

川
river
chuān

金
gold
jīn

characters

opposites

大
big
dà

小
small
xiǎo

上
up
shàng

下
down
xià

city

京
capital
jīng

transport

舟
boat
zhōu

車
car
chē

I spy with my little eye ...
... a Chinese character on these pages that looks like three pointy fingers.
Can you guess the answer?

go to **page 80** for the answer

numbers

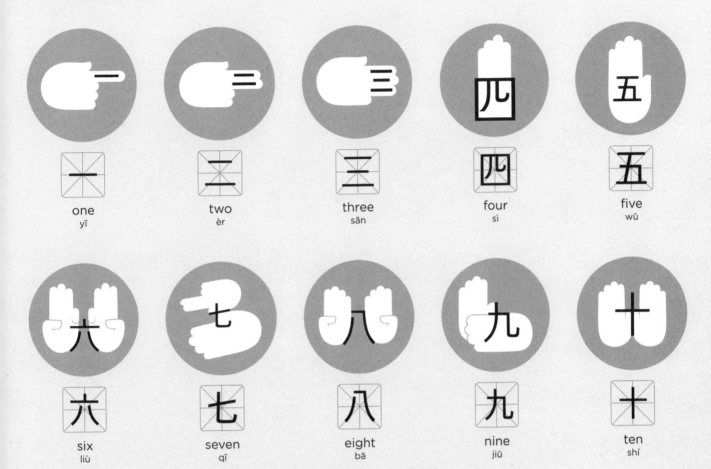

one
yī

two
èr

three
sān

four
sì

five
wǔ

six
liù

seven
qī

eight
bā

nine
jiǔ

ten
shí

counting to 20

The numbers 11 to 19 all start with the number 10, which is 十 in Chinese. This is how it works:

11	10 (十) + 1 (一) = 十一	**16**	10 (十) + 6 (六) = 十六
12	10 (十) + 2 (二) = 十二	**17**	10 (十) + 7 (七) = 十七
13	10 (十) + 3 (三) = 十三	**18**	10 (十) + 8 (八) = 十八
14	10 (十) + 4 (四) = 十四	**19**	10 (十) + 9 (九) = 十九
15	10 (十) + 5 (五) = 十五	**20**	2 (二) × 10 (十) = 二十

phrases

When two characters sit next to each other,
they make a phrase, which has a new meaning.
A phrase fits into two or more writing boxes.

people

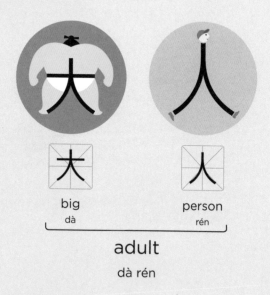

大
big
dà

人
person
rén

adult
dà rén

人
person
rén

鱼
fish
yú

mermaid
rén yú

nature

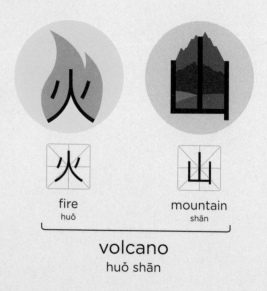

火
fire
huǒ

山
mountain
shān

volcano
huǒ shān

雨
rain
yǔ

林
woods
lín

rain forest
yǔ lín

planets

土
soil
tǔ

星
star
xīng

Saturn
tǔ xīng

木
tree
mù

星
star
xīng

Jupiter
mù xīng

火
fire
huǒ

星
star
xīng

Mars
huǒ xīng

Earth
dì qiú

Earth is made up of two characters. The first means land. The second means round like a ball. Together it means a ball of land.

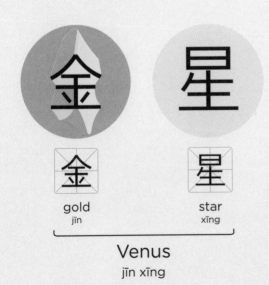

金
gold
jīn

星
star
xīng

Venus
jīn xīng

水
water
shuǐ

星
star
xīng

Mercury
shuǐ xīng

notes for parents and teachers

What's the Chineasy approach for children?

Chineasy is a simple and playful introduction to written Chinese. It can be fun to start by simply looking up everyday words. Next study the pictures closely and pick out memorable details about the shape of each character. Encourage children to make up their own stories to remember the characters by and play guessing games to test their knowledge.

Children will soon become familiar with some basic characters and will then be able to recognise compound characters and phrases too.

What's traditional and simplified Chinese?

Traditional Chinese is the form of written Chinese that hasn't changed for thousands of years. Simplified Chinese was introduced in 1949 to help promote mass literacy with characters that are easier to read and write. Many traditional and simplified characters share the same form and look identical.

In this book, characters are shown in the form easiest for beginners to understand, often the most visual. See the box below for more detail.

traditional characters

Here are the traditional characters from this book that don't look the same in their simplified form.

bird
traditional 鳥
simplified 鸟

duck
traditional 鴨
simplified 鸭

pig
traditional 豬
simplified 猪

car
traditional 車
simplified 车

fish
traditional 魚
simplified 鱼

shell
traditional 貝
simplified 贝

cat
traditional 貓
simplified 猫

horse
traditional 馬
simplified 马

turtle
traditional 龜
simplified 龟

Does this book help children speak Chinese?

The main aim of this book is to introduce children to written Chinese and familiarise them with the characters. When children are beginners, they will enjoy having a go at speaking but it's not necessary to focus on perfect pronunciation, especially if you are not a Chinese-speaker yourself. Encourage children to have fun making different sounds and playing with their voice and intonation. Once they are familiar with some words, then concentrate on speaking out loud with the correct pronunciation.

The following link is useful for teachers and parents to find out how Chinese is pronounced chineasy.com/talk/lessons/002-the-tones

What is a tonal language?

Chinese is a tonal language, which means when a syllable is pronounced in a different tone, it produces a different meaning.

Is Chineasy based on Mandarin Chinese?

Yes. In China, Mandarin is the most widely spoken dialect, or regional variety of the language. Out of a total of 1.2 billion native speakers about 960 million speak Mandarin.

Is Chinese read horizontally or vertically?

Traditionally Chinese writing was always written in columns and read from top to bottom. Today, Chinese can also be written in rows and read from left to right, the same way as English.

What about writing in Chinese?

In this book, every character is presented in a 'writing box' showing the exact shape of each stroke.

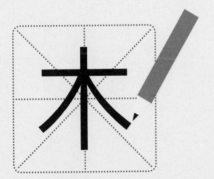

How is pronunciation shown?

This book uses a phonetic system called pinyin, which spells out the sound of Chinese characters in the English language.

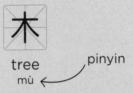

tree   pinyin
mù ←

Look at the mark, or tone, attached to each pinyin. This shows which of the four tones to use to pronounce the word in Chinese.

first tone – high and level
For example, say, 'Ahhhh!' as if you are at the dentist.

second tone – starts low and goes up
For example, say, 'What?!'

third tone – starts flat, falls, then rises
For example, say, 'Really?' like you don't believe something.

fourth tone – starts high then falls
For example, say, 'NO!' with an angry voice.

index

index

answers

page 10 follow the clues

page 19 top to toe

 I kick a football with my **foot**.

I lick an ice-cream with my **tongue**.

I hold a pencil in my **hand**.

page 25 balloon spotting

I wear a hat and I'm spooky.
I am a **witch** on the orange balloon.

I'm the only one without a hat.
I am a **ghost** on the purple balloon.

page 27 Who's where?

big is in the **down** lift

page 37 Guess who?

I make my home inside a hard brown
shell with a pattern on top.
I am a **turtle**.

We are the same kind of animal.
We both have feathers.
We are **duck** and **bird**.

page 49 star spotting

 fire star **Mars**   water star **Mercury**

 soil star **Saturn**   gold star **Venus**

page 52 let's explore

page 57 postcard match-up

page 61 party match-up

pages 65 I spy   **pages 67 I spy**

pages 69 I spy   **pages 70 I spy**

First published in the United Kingdom in 2018 by Thames & Hudson Ltd, 181A High Holborn, London WC1V 7QX

Elements from this book were first published in *Chineasy* (2014) and *Chineasy Everyday* (2016).

Chineasy for Children © 2018 Chineasy Ltd (chineasy.com)

'Chineasy' is a registered word and logo trademark of ShaoLan Hsueh, used under licence by Thames & Hudson Ltd.

Author: ShaoLan Hsueh
Illustrator: Noma Bar
Editor and copywriter: Jane Wilsher
Designer: Belinda Webster

The right of ShaoLan Hsueh to be identified as the author of this Work has been asserted by her in accordance with the Copyright, Designs and Patents Act 1988.

British Library Cataloguing-in-Publication Data

A catalogue record for this book is available from the British Library

ISBN 978-0-500-65121-6

Printed & bound in China by C&C Offset Printing Co Ltd

To find out about all our publications, please visit
www.thamesandhudson.com.
There you can subscribe to our e-newsletter, browse or download our current catalogue, and buy any titles that are in print.